9/92

Klee *as in* clay

A Pronunciation Guide

**Compiled, written and edited
by Wilfred J. McConkey**

Contents

Published by Madison Books
4720 Boston Way
Lanham, Maryland 20706

3 Henrietta Street
London WC2E 8LU England

Distributed by National Book Network

The paper used in this publication meets the minimum
requirements of American National Standard for
Information Sciences—Permanence of Paper for
Printed Library Materials, ANSI Z39.48–1984.   ™
Manufactured in the United States of America.

Library of Congress Cataloging-in-Publication Data

McConkey, Wilfred J.
Klee as in clay : a pronunciation guide / compiled,
written, and edited by Wilfred J. McConkey. —3rd ed.
p.   cm.
Includes index.
1. Artists—Registers.   2. Names—Pronunciation.
I. Title.
NX163.M3   1991
700'.92' 2—dc20   91-26863 CIP
ISBN 0–8191–8247–8 (pbk. : alk. paper)

British Cataloging in Publication Information Available

Introduction

One of the most satisfying changes we made in preparing this edition was striking "HAVEL, Václav" from the Literature and Drama roster. His second career as a head of state brought him celebrity's highest reward: his name enunciated correctly and frequently on newscasts the world over. As a result the Czech playwrite soon forfeited his most-frequently-mispronounced status in America.

On the other hand, "VARGAS LLOSA, Mario" stays. This was an arguable call, but fame and name association are fleeting for failed candidates for Latin American presidencies. Moreover, his name presents a much greater challenge to the unwary than Havel's.

It's quite conceivable that if these important contributors to Western culture hadn't made excursions into politics their legions of admirers in North American might never have heard either name mentioned on radio or TV (unless they listened assiduously to National Public Radio or Canada's CBC Network). Benign or not, the electronic media's neglect of the arts, except for music, is one reason the illustrious names in this guide continue to be mispronounced by otherwise well-informed people.

Another reason is that most of the names are "foreign." This holds true, of course, from whatever national perspective they're viewed, since no country has a corner on creativity or virtuosity. In a nation of immigrants, however, the problem is compounded. Edward Ruscha (roo-*shay*) is an American painter, yet his compatriots enjoy no home-field advantage in figuring out how to pronounce his name.

The standard for pronunciations in this guide is acceptance by knowledgeable Americans. Who are these mavens? Generally people who, in practicing their professions, have occasion to use the names regularly in conversation. They include art curators, gallery staffs, publicists for book publishers and recording companies, cultural attachés, music columnists, agency reps for performing artists and faculty members of literature departments and fine arts and architecture schools.

Sometimes they are simply the most knowledgeable sources, whatever their nationality. Czeław Miłosz, the Polish poet and novelist now teaching in the U.S., diagrammed the version of his name he hears most often from American colleagues. Lawrence Durrell, the recently-deceased English novelist, okayed the guide's rendering of his surname, and provided what promised to be the definitive pronunciation of his long-time friend Anaïs Nin's first name. (Oddly enough, as a reader subsequently pointed out, it's different from the one she offers in her autobiography. This edition recognizes both versions.) The daughter of Spanish poet Jorge Guillén wrote to correct a vowel sound in the guide's rendering of his name.

For most foreign names in this guide the country-of-origin pronunciation works at home and abroad. Among the exceptions are names, often of emigrés, whose pronunciation has been "naturalized." Huysmans, for instance, was of Dutch descent and Brancusi was Romanian, but both flourished creatively—as a writer and sculptor, respectively—in Paris. As a result the French pronunciation of their names is the most widely accepted.

Americans stripped composer Kurt Weill and author Elie Wiesel of their VWs after they settled in the U.S. But Richard Wagner, Carl Maria von Weber and Anton von Webern, who remained in Europe, were allowed to keep theirs.

The pronunciation of some names, Bach and van Gogh for example, has been modified to eliminate sounds Americans aren't accustomed to producing. You may ingratiate yourself with fellow concert-goers in Leipzig by pronouncing Bach with an explosive *"b"* but if you try it at home you'll just sound pretentious.

The revisions made for this edition include corrections like the ones mentioned above, and refinements in pronunciation instructions to reduce ambiguity and improve felicity (Wouk rendered as *woke* rather than *wohk*). Six names, judged either too obscure or too prominent, were dropped. Thirty-four names have been added, most because they've become widely known since the first edition appeared, and others because they should have been in all along.

Wilfred J. McConkey
Grosse Pointe, Michigan
August, 1991

Pronunciation keys

- Pronunciations appear in parentheses.
- Boldface type indicates emphasis.
- Common words are used whenever possible to indicate how a name, or a part of a name, should be pronounced. Phonetic spellings are used only when words fail.

If a combination of letters spells a common word, like *me* or *knee* for example, it is the sound of that word that's called for.

- When a letter combination isn't immediately recognizable as a common word, treat it as phonetic spelling.
- A *zh* indicates the sound of the *z* in *azure*.

Architecture

ANTES, Horst
(**on**•tes)

> *b. 1936*
> *German architect*

BREUER, Marcel
(**broy**•ur)

> *b. 1902*
> *Hungarian-American architect*

BRUNELLESCHI, Filippo
(brew•nell•**less**•key)

> *1377–1446*
> *Florentine architect*

CANDELA, Felix
(con•**day**•la)

> *b. 1910*
> *Mexican architect*

CUVILLIÉS, Francois
(cue•vee•**ess**)

> *1695–1768*
> *Walloon architect*

CUYPERS, Petrus
(**coy**•purse)

> *1827–1921*
> *Dutch architect*

EAMES, Charles
(**eems**)

> *1907–1978*
> *American designer and architect*

GAUDÍ, Antonio
(gow•**dee**)

> *1852–1926*
> *Spanish architect*

GILLY, Friedrich
(zhil•ee)

1772–1800
German architect

GIURGOLA, Romaldo
(joor•go•la)

b. 1920
American architect

GOERITZ, Mathias
(gur•its)

b. 1951
German sculptor and architect living in Mexico

GROPIUS, Walter
(grow•pee•us, valter)

1883–1969
German architect

GRUEN, Victor
(grewen)

1903–1980
Austrian-born American architect

GUIMARD, Hector
(gee [as in geek]•mar, ek•tor)

1867–1942
French architect

HARDOUIN-MANSART, Jules
(ar•dwan, mansahr)

1646–1704
French architect

HAUSSMAN, George Eugène, Baron
(owes•mon)

1809–1891
French urban planner

HEJDUK, John
(hay•duke)

b. 1929
American architect

HERRERA, Juan de
(ay•**ray**•rah)

1530–1597
Spanish architect

HOLLEIN, Hans
(**haul**•yun)

b. 1934
Austrian architect

JEKYLL, Gertrude
(jeekle)

1843–1932
English landscape architect

JOCOBSEN, Arne
(**yaw**•cope•sen, **ar**•nuh)

1902–1971
Danish architect

KIESLER, Frederick John
(**keys**•lur)

1896–1965
Austrian architect

LeCORBUSIER
(core•boozy•**ay**)

1887–1965   Born Charles Edouard Jeanneret
Swiss-French architect

LOOS, Adolf
(lows)

1870–1933
Austrian architect

LUTYENS, Sir Edwin Landseer
(luchenz)

1869–1944
British architect

MIES VAN DER ROHE, Ludwig
(mees•van•dare•**roe**•uh, **loot**•vic)

1886–1969
German architect

OUD, Jacobus Johannes Pieter
(oat)

1890–1963
Dutch architect

PEI, I. M.
(pay)

b. 1917
Chinese-American architect

PERRET, Auguste
(pair•ay)

1874–1954
French architect

ROCHE, Kevin
(roach)

b. 1922
Irish-born architect

VAUX, Calvert
(vox)

1824–1895
English architect who emigrated to the U.S.

Literature and Drama

AGEE, James
(ay•jee)

1909–1955
American poet, novelist, essayist and screenwriter

ALEICHEM, Sholem
(a•leh•hem)

1859–1916
Pen name of Solomon Rabinowitz, Ukranian-born Yiddish novelist, playwright and short-story writer

ALLENDE, Isabel
(a•yen•day)

b. 1942
Chilean novelist

ANGELL, Roger
(angel)

b. 1920
American writer and editor

ANOUILH, Jean
(ah•new•ee)

b. 1910
French dramatist

BARTHELME, Donald
(bar•tull•me)

1931–1989
American novelist and short-story writer

BARTHES, Roland
(bart)

1915–1980
French literary critic and essayist

BATAILLE, Henry
(bah•tie)

1872–1922
French dramatist

BAUDELAIRE, Charles
(bode•**lair**)

1821–1867
French poet

BECHER, Johannes
(**besh**•ur)

1891–1958
German poet

BOCCACCIO, Giovanni
(bo•**caw**•cho)

1313–1375
Italian novelist

BÖLL, Heinrich
(burl [preferably with a silent r])

1917–1985   German author, winner of the Nobel
Prize for literature in 1972

BORGES, Jorge Luis
(**bore**•hays, **hoar**•hay, loo•ease)

1889–1986
Argentinian poet and essayist

BRECHT, Bertold
(brekht, **bare**•told)

1898–1956
German poet and playwright

BRETON, André
(bre•**tone**)

1896–1966
French poet, essayist, critic and editor

BRIEUX, Eugène
(bree•**oo**)

1858–1932
French dramatist

BROUN, Heywood
(broon)

1888–1939
American newspaper columnist

BUZZATI, Dino
(boo•**tsah**•tee)

1906–1972
Italian novelist and playwright

CABELL, James B.
(**cab**•ull)

1879–1958
American novelist

CAEDMON
(**cad**•mun)

about 670
Thought to be the first English poet

CAHAN, Abraham
(con)

1850–1951   Russian-American journalist and
novelist. Edited Jewish Daily Forward in
New York City

CAMMAERTS, Émile
(**caw**•marts)

1878–1953
Belgian poet

CAMUS, Albert
(cam•**oo**, al•**bear**)

1913–1960   Algerian-born French novelist,
essayist and playwright

CAPEK, Karel
(**chaw**•peck)

1890–1938
Czech playwright who coined the word robot

CAPOTE, Truman
(ka•**po**•tee)

1924–1984
American novelist, journalist

CATHER, Willa
(as in Catherine)

1873–1947
American novelist

CAVAFY, C. P.
(caw•**vaw**•fee)

1863–1933
Greek poet

CHAYEFSKY, Paddy
(chy•**ev**•ski)

1923–1981
American playwright and screenwriter

CIARDI, John
(chee•**are**•dee)

1916–1986
American poet

CLAUS, Hugo
(cloze)

b. 1929
Flemish poet, playwright, novelist and film writer

CLAUSEWITZ, Carl Philipp Gottfried von
(rhymes with **ploughs**•a•vits)

1780–1831
Prussian general and writer on warfare

CLOETE, Stuart
(clooty)

1897–1976
South African novelist, poet and biographer

COCTEAU, Jean
(cock•**toe**)

1889–1963   French novelist, playwright, poet,
painter, designer and film maker

COETZEE, John
(rhymes with put•zee)

b. 1940
African novelist

CORNEILLE, Pierre
(core•**nay**)

1606–1684
French dramatist

COZZENS, James Gould
(cousins)

1903–1978
American novelist

CREASEY, John
(**cree**•zee)

1908–1973
English mystery writer

CRÉBILLON, Prosper de
(cray•bee•**own**)

1674–1762
French dramatist

DaPONTE, Lorenzo
(dah•**pawn**•tay)

1749–1838
Italian poet and librettist

D'ANNUNZIO, Gabriele
(don•**noont**•see•oh, gabree•**ay**•lay)

1863–1938
Italian poet, playwright, novelist and patriot

DANTE, Alighieri
(**don**•tay, olly•**gyay**•ree)

1265–1321
Italian poet

DAUDET, Alphonse
(doe•**day**)

1840–1897
French novelist, dramatist and short-story writer

DeKRUIF, Paul
(da•**kreef**)

1890–1971
American author and bacteriologist

DIDEROT, Denis
(deed•**roe**, duh•knee)

1713–1784
French philosopher, essayist and critic

DINESEN, Isak
(**dee**•nuh•sun, **ee**•sock)

1885–1962
Danish author

DIOP, David
(dee•**ope**)

1927–1960
African poet

DOS PASSOS, John
(dose•**pass**•us)

1896–1970
American novelist

DREISER, Theodore
(**dry**•sir)

1871–1945
American novelist

DUHAMEL, George
(do•ah•**mell**, zhorzh)

1884–1966
French novelist and poet

DUMAS, Alexandre
(do•**maw**)

1802–1870
French novelist

DURAS, Marguerite
(due•**rah**)

b. 1914
French novelist

DURRELL, Laurence
(durl)

1912–1990
English novelist, poet, essayist and travel writer

DÜRRENMATT, Friedrich
(**dour**•en•mott)

1921–1990
Swiss novelist and playwright

ECO, Umberto
(echo, oom•**bare**•toe)

b. 1932
Italian author and professor of Semiotics

EHRENBURG, Ilya Grigorievich
(**ay**•ren•boork, eelya)

1891–1967
Russian journalist and novelist

ÉLUARD, Paul
(ay•loo•**ar**)

1895–1952
French poet

FARQUE, Léon Paul
(farg)

1876–1947
French poet

FEDIN, Konstantin Aleksandrovich
(**feh**•jin)

1892–1977
Russian novelist

FEUCHTWANGER, Lion
(**foysht**•vonger, **lee**•own)

1884–1958
German novelist and playwright

FEYDEAU, George
(fay•**doe**, zhorzh)

1862–1921
French dramatist

FLAUBERT, Gustave
(flow•**bare**)

1821–1880
French novelist

FOWLES, John
(**fouls**)

b. 1926
English novelist

FRANCE, Anatole
(fronce)

1844–1924
French novelist, poet and critic

FRÉCHETTE, Louis Honoré
(fray•shet)

1839–1908
French-Canadian poet

GARCÍA LORCA, Frederico
(gar•thia)

1898–1936
Spanish poet and dramatist

GARCIA MÁRQUEZ, Gabriel
(mar•kez, ga•bree•el)

b. 1928
Columbian novelist, winner of the Nobel Prize for
literature.

GENET, Jean
(zhuh•nay, zhon)

1910–1986
French novelist and playwright

GEORGE, Stefan
(gay•or•guh, shtef•on)

1868–1933
German poet

GIDE, André
(zheed, ondray)

1869–1951
French novelist and playwright

GIONO, Jean
(joe•no)

1895–1970
French novelist

GIRAUDOUX, Jean
(zhee•roe•do, zhon)

1882–1944
French playwright and diplomat

GJELLERUP, Karl Adolph
(yell•ur•up)

1857–1919
Danish novelist and poet

GOETHE, Johann Wolfgang von
(gerta [preferably with a silent r])

1749–1832
German poet and novelist

GOGOL, Nikolai
(go•gull)

1809–1852
Russian novelist

GRASS, Günter
(graws, **gun**•tur)

b. 1927
German novelist, poet and playwright

GRAU, Shirley Ann
(grow)

b. 1929
American novelist and short-story writer

GRILLPARZER, Franz
(**grill**•part•sir, frahnts)

1791–1872
Austrian dramatist

GUILLÉN, Jorge
(geel•**yen**, hoar•hay)

1893–1984
Spanish poet

GUITRY, Sacha
(gee [as in geek]•**tree**, saw•**shaw**)

1885–1957
French dramatist, producer and actor

HANDKE, Peter
(**hond**•kuh, **pay**•ter)

b. 1942
Austrian novelist and dramatist

HARTOG, Jan de
(**har•**tock, yawn)

b. 1914
Dutch-English playwright and novelist

HEARN, Lafcadio
(laugh•**kay•**dio)

1850–1904
Irish-Greek writer

HÉBERT, Anne
(ay•bare)

b. 1916
French-Canadian poet, novelist and playwright

HEIJERMANS, Herman
(**higher•**mons)

1864–1924
Dutch novelist, journalist and playwright

HEINE, Heinrich
(**hine•**uh, **hine•**rick)

1797–1856
German poet

HESSE, Herman
(**hess•**uh)

1877–1962
German-Swiss novelist and poet

HOCHHUTH, Rolf
(hawk•hoot)

b. 1931
German dramatist

HUYSMANS, George Charles
(weez-mons, zhorge sharl)

1848–1907
French novelist and art critic of Dutch descent

IONESCO, Eugène
(ee•oh•**ness•**co, oo•zhen)

b. 1912
Romanian-born playwright

JARREL, Randall
(jair•ul)

1914–1965
American poet

JARRY, Alfred
(zhah•ree)

1873–1907
French dramatist, poet and humorist

KAFKA, Franz
(cough•ka)

1883–1924
Czech novelist

KAZIN, Alfred
(kay•zin)

b. 1915 American literary critic, editor and autobiographer

KESEY, Ken
(key•zee)

b. 1935
American novelist

KOESTLER, Arthur
(kest•lur)

1905–1983
Hungarian-born novelist and science writer

KOSINSKI, Jerzy
(kuh•zin•ski, yur•zee)

1933–1991
Polish-born novelist

KUNDERA, Milan
(coon•dura, me•lawn)

b. 1929
Czech novelist

MAETERLINCK, Maurice
(mah•tur•lonk, mo•reese)

1862–1949
Belgian poet, dramatist and essayist

MAHFOUZ, Naguib
(ma•fooz, na•**geeb**)

b. 1911
Egyptian novelist

MALLET-JORIS, Francoise
(mall•**ay**, zhor•ee, frahn•swahz)

b. 1930
Belgian novelist

MALRAUX, André
(mal•**roe**)

1901–1976
French novelist

MAMET, David
(**ma**•mit)

b. 1947
American playwright

MARSH, Edith Ngaio
(**nigh**•oh)

1899–1982
New Zealand-born detective-story writer

MICKIEWICZ, Adam
(**mick**•uh•vich)

1798–1855
Polish poet

MIŁOSZ, Czeław
(**me**•losh, **cres**•love)

b. 1911   Polish poet and novelist, now a
naturalized U.S. citizen. Won Nobel Prize for
literature in 1980.

MISTRAL, Frédéric
(mees•**trawl**, fray•day•**reek**)

1830–1914
French poet

MONTALE, Eugenio
(moan•**taw**•lay, ay•oo•**jen**•yo)

1896–1981   Italian essayist and poet, winner of
the Nobel Prize for literature in 1975

MONTHERLANT, Henri de
(moan•tare•**lawn**)

1896–1972
French novelist and dramatist

MUSSET, Alfred de
(mew•**say**)

1810–1857
French poet and playwright

NOBOKOV, Vladimir
(na•**baw**•cawv, vlud•**ee**•mir)

1899–1977
Russian-born novelist

NAIPAUL, V. S.
(nigh•paul)

b. 1932
Trinidad-born novelist of Indian parentage

NIN, Anaïs
(anna•eece or anna•ease)

1903–1977
American novelist and diarist

O'FAOLAIN, Sean
(oh•**fway**•lon, shawn)

1900–1991
Irish novelist and short-story writer

ORTEGA Y GASSET, José
(or•**tay**•gah ee gah•**set**)

1883–1955
Spanish essayist and philosopher

PAGNOL, Marcel
(pawn•**yoll**)

1895–1974
French dramatist, film writer and director

PATER, Walter
(**pay**•tur)

1839–1894
British literary critic and essayist

PAZ, Octavio
(paws)

b. 1914
Mexican poet, essayist and literary critic

PEPYS, Samuel
(peeps)

1633–1703
English diarist and public servant

PERSE, Saint-John
(pairs)

1887–1975   French poet and diplomat who won
the Nobel Prize for literature in 1960. Real name:
Aléxis Saint-Léger Léger

PROUST, Marcel
(proost)

1871–1922
French novelist

PUIG, Manuel
(poy•eeg)

1932–1990
Argentine writer

RABELAIS, Francois
(rab•lay)

1494–1553
French satirical novelist

RAND, Ayn
(ayn rhymes with nine)

1905–1983   Russian-born American novelist,
dramatist and essayist

REMARQUE, Erich Maria
(ruh•mark)

1898–1970
German-born novelist

RHYS, Jean
(reece)

1894–1979
English novelist

RILKE, Rainer Maria
(**rill**•cuh, **rye**•nur)

1875–1926
German poet

RIMBAUD, Arthur
(ram•**bo**)

1854–1891
French poet

ROBBE-GRILLET, Alain
(robe•gree•**ay**)

b. 1922
French novelist and screenwriter

ROETHKE, Theodore
(**ret**•cuh)

1908–1963
American poet

ROMAINS, Jules
(roe•**man**)

1885–1972   French playwright and novelist. Real name: Louis Farigoule

ROY, Gabrielle
(rwah)

b. 1909
French-Canadian novelist

SAINTE-BEUVE, Charles Augustin
(sant•**buv**, sharl)

1804–1869
French literary critic

SAKI
(**saw**•key)

1870–1916   Pen name for Hector Hugh Munro. British satirist and humorist

SARRAUTE, Nathalie
(saw•**rote**)

b. 1902
Russian-born French novelist and playwright

SARTRE, Jean Paul
(**sahr**•truh)

1905–1980
French philosopher, social critic and author

SCRIBE, Augustin
(screeb)

1791–1861
French playwright

SHAFFER, Peter
(**shaf**•ur)

b. 1926
British dramatist

SILONE, Ignazio
(see•**low**•nay)

1900–1978   Pen name of Secondo Tranquilli,
Italian novelist and anti-Facist activist

SOLZHENITSYN, Aleksandr
(soul•zhuh•**neet**•sin)

b. 1918   Expatriate Russian novelist, winner of
the Nobel Prize for literature in 1970

STAËL, Madame de
(stall)

1766–1817
Swiss-French novelist and literary critic

STENDHAL
(stan•**doll**)

1783–1842
Pen name of Marie-Henri Beyle, French novelist

STRACHEY, Lytton
(**stray**•chee, littun)

1880–1932
English biographer

SYNGE, John Millington
(**sing**)

1871–1909
Irish playwright

TALESE, Gay
(tal•**ease**)

> *b. 1932*
> *American reporter and author*

THOMAS, Dylan
(dillon)

> *1914–1953*
> *Welsh poet*

TOCQUEVILLE, Alexis de
(toke•**veal**)

> *1805–1859*
> *French author of Democracy in America*

TOLKIEN, J. R. R.
(**toll**•keen)

> *1892–1973*
> *British author*

TUCHMAN, Barbara
(**tuck**•man)

> *1912–1989*
> *American historian, winner of two Pulitzer Prizes*

TURGENEV, Ivan
(tour•**gain**•yif)

> *1818–1883*
> *Russian novelist and short-story writer*

VALÉRY, Paul
(vuh•lay•**ree**)

> *1871–1945*
> *French poet*

VARGAS LLOSA, Mario
(yosa)

> *b. 1936*
> *Peruvian novelist*

VERLAINE, Paul
(vair•**len**)

> *1844–1896*
> *French poet*

VILLON, Francois
(vee•yohn)

> *1431–1463*
> *French poet*

WEDEKIND, Frank
(vay•de•kint)

> *1864–1913*
> *German poet and playwright*

WEISS, Peter
(vice)

> *b. 1916*
> *German playwright, novelist and film director*

WERFEL, Franz
(**vair•**full)

> *1890–1945*
> *Austrian novelist and playwright*

WIESEL, Eliezer "Elie"
(we•**zell**)

> *b. 1928*
> *Romanian-born American author*

WOUK, Herman
(woke)

> *b. 1915*
> *American novelist*

YEATS, William Butler
(yates)

> *1865–1939*
> *Irish poet and dramatist*

ZWEIG, Stefan
(tsvike)

> *1881–1942*
> *Austrian writer*

Music and Dance

ALBANESE, Licia
(all•bah•**nay**•zay, **lee**•chaw)

b. 1913
Italian-American soprano

ARRAU, Claudio
(rhymes with allow)

1903–1991
*Chilean pianist (Spanish: are **rah**•oo)*

BACH, Johann Sebastian
(bock)

1735–1782
German composer

BACKHAUS, Wilhelm
(**bock**•hows)

1884–1969
German pianist

BALANCHINE, George
(**bal**•uncheen)

1904–1983
Russian-born choreographer

BARYSHNIKOV, Mikhail
(buh•**rish**•knee•cough, meek•hyle)

b. 1948
Latvian-born ballet dancer and director

BERNSTEIN, Leonard
(burn•stine)

1918–1990
American composer and conductor

BÖHM, Karl
(burm [preferably with a silent r])

1894–1981
Austrian conductor

BOIELDIEU, Francois Adrien
(bwah•el•**due**)

1775–1834
French opera composer

BOITO, Arrigo
(bo•**ee**•toe)

1842–1918
Italian composer and librettist

BOULEZ, Pierre
(boo•**lez**)

b. 1925
French composer and conductor

BRUCH, Max
(brook)

1838–1920
German composer

BRUHN, Erik
(broon)

1928–1986
Danish ballet dancer and director

BUJONES, Fernando
(boo•**hoe**•nays)

b. 1955
American ballet dancer

BUXTEHUDE, Dietrich
(**bucks**•tuh•hoo•dee)

1637–1707
Danish-born organist and composer

CASADESUS, Robert
(casod•soos, ro•**bare**)

1899–1972
French pianist and composer

CASTELNUOVO-TEDESCO, Mario
(tay•**days**•co)

1895–1968
Italian-American composer

CHABRIER, Emmanuell
(shaw•bree•**ay**)

1841–1894
French composer

CHALIAPIN, Fyodor Ivanovich
(shawly•**awp**•in)

1873–1938
Russian basso

CHAMINADE, Cécile
(shaw•me•**nod**)

1857–1944
French pianist and composer

CHARPENTIER, Gustave
(shar•pon•**tee/ay**)

1860–1956
French composer

CHAUSSON, Ernest
(show•**sawn**)

1855–1899
French composer

CHÁVEZ, Carlos
(**shaw**•vays)

1899–1978
Mexican composer

CHERUBINI, Luigi
(care•uh•**beanie**)

1760–1842
Italian composer

CILEÁ, Francesco
(chee•**lay**•ah)

1866–1950
Italian composer

CIMAROSA, Domenico
(chee•ma•**row**•zah)

1749–1801
Italian opera composer

CORTOT, Alfred
(core•**toe**)

1877–1962
French pianist

COUPERIN, Francois
(coo•per•**an**)

1668–1733
French composer and organist

CZERNY, Carl
(**chair**•knee)

1791–1857
Austrian composer, pianist and teacher

d'AMBOISE, Jacques
(dom•**bwahz**)

b. 1934
American ballet dancer

DANILOVA, Alexandra
(da•**knee**•lowva)

b. 1904
Russian-born ballerina and teacher

DAVID, Félicien César
(daw•**veed**, fay•lee•see•**an**)

1810–1876
French composer

DEBUSSY, Claude
(deb•you•**see**)

1862–1918
French composer

DELIBES, Léo
(duh•**leeb**, **lay**•oh)

1836–1891
French composer

DELLO JOIO, Norman
(**joyo**)

b. 1913
American composer

DIAGHILEV, Serge Pavlovich
(**dee•ah•gill•**yeff, sir•gay)

1872–1929
Russian ballet impressario

DIMITROVA, Ghena
(dee•**me•**trova, gaina)

b. 1941
Bulgarian soprano

DOHNÁNYI, Ernst von
(daw•**non•**yee, airnst fan)

1877–1960
Hungarian composer, pianist and teacher

DVOŘÁK, Antonin
(**dvor•**zhock)

1841–1904
Bohemian composer

FALLA, Manuel de
(**fah•**yuh, man•**well**)

1876–1946
Spanish composer

FAURÉ, Gabriel Urbain
(for•ay, gah•bree•**el** your•**ban**)

1845–1924
French composer

FISHER-DIESKAU, Dietrick
(fisher **deese•**cow, deet•rick)

b. 1925
German baritone

FOSS, Lukas
(faws)

b. 1922   German-born American composer,
conductor and pianist

FRACCI, Carla
(fraught•chee)

b. 1936
Italian ballerina

FRANCESCATTI, Zino
(fron•chess•**cot**•ee)

b. 1905
French violinist

FRANCK, César
(fronk, say•**zar**)

1822–1890
Belgian composer

FURTWÄNGLER, Wilhelm
(**foort**•veng•glur)

1886–1954
German conductor

GIGLI, Beniamino
(**jeel**•yee, ben•yah•**mean**•oh)

1890–1957
Italian tenor

GINASTERA, Alberto
(hee•nah•**stay**•rah)

b. 1916
Argentine composer

GIORDANO, Umberto
(johr•**don**•o)

1867–1948
Italian composer

GLIÈRE, Rheinhold Moritzovich
(glee•**air**)

1875–1956
Russian composer and conductor

GODUNOV, Aleksandr
(**go**•duh•noff)

b. 1950
Soviet dancer who defected to the U.S. in 1979

GOUNOD, Charles
(goo•**no**, sharl)

1818–1893
French composer

HAITINK, Bernard
(**high**•tink)

b. 1929
Dutch conductor

HALÉVY, Jacques
(ah•lay•**vee**)

1799–1862
French composer

HAYDN, Franz Josef
(**high**•dn)

1732–1809
Austrian composer

HENZE, Hans Werner
(hent•see, hahns **vair**•nur)

b. 1926
German composer

HONNEGGER, Arthur
(oh•nay•**gair**, artoor)

1892–1955
French composer

IBERT, Jacques
(ee•**bare**)

1890–1962
French composer

d'INDY, Vincent
(dan•**dee**, van•**sawn**)

1855–1931
French composer

ITURBI, José
(ee•**tour**•bee, hoe•**zay**)

1895–1980
Spanish-born pianist and conductor

JANÁČEK, Leoš
(**yawn**•ah•check, **lay**•ohsh)

1854–1928
Czech composer

JERITZA, Maria
(yuh•**rits**•uh)

> *1887–1982*
> *Czech soprano*

JOACHIM, Joseph
(**yoh**•ah•kim, **yoh**•sef)

> *1831–1907*
> *Hungarian violinist and composer*

JOLIVET, André
(zhoh•lee•vay, on•**dray**)

> *1905–1974*
> *French composer*

JOOSS, Kurt
(yohs, coort)

> *1901–1979*
> *German choreographer*

KARAJAN, Herbert von
(**car**•ah•yawn)

> *1908–1989*
> *Austrian conductor*

KÖCHEL, Ludwig Ritter von
(curshle [preferably with a silent r])

> *1800–1877*   *Austrian music bibliographer who*
> *catalogued Mozart's works*

KODÁLY, Zoltán
(co•**dye**)

> *1882–1967*
> *Hungarian composer*

KREUTZER, Rodolphe
(crut•**sair**)

> *1766–1831*   *French violinist and composer of*
> *German extraction*

LALO, Édouard
(law•**low**)

> *1823–1892*
> *French composer*

LIFAR, Serge
(lee•**far**, sir•gay)

1905–1986
Russian-born dancer and ballet master

LULLY, Jean Baptiste
(loo•**lee**)

1632–1687
Italian-born French composer

MASCAGNI, Pietro
(mahs•**con**•yee)

1863–1945
Italian composer

MESSIAEN, Olivier
(messy•**on**, oh•liv•ee•**ay**)

b. 1908
French composer

MILHAUD, Darius
(me•**oh**)

1892–1974
French composer

MUNCH, Charles
(moonsh, sharl)

1891–1968   German-born orchestra conductor
long associated with the Boston Symphony
Orchestra

NIJINSKA, Bronislava
(knee•**zhin**•ska)

1891–1972   Russian-born ballet dancer and
choreographer, sister of Vaslav

NIJINSKY, Vaslav
(knee•**zhin**•ski)

1888–1950
Russian-born ballet dancer and choreographer

NUREYEV, Rudolf
(nuh•**ray**•ef)

b. 1938
Russian-born ballet dancer

OFFENBACH, Jacques
(**aw**•fen•bok)

1819–1880
German-born composer of French operettas

OZAWA, Seiji
(oh•**zah**•wah, **say**•jee)

b. 1935
Manchurian-born Japanese orchestra conductor

PACHELBEL, Johann
(**paw**•cull•bell)

1653–1706
German composer and organist

PADEREWSKI, Ignace Jan
(podder•**ef**•ski)

1860–1941
Polish statesman, composer and pianist

PAISIELLO, Giovanni
(paw•ease•ee•**el**•low)

1740–1816
Italian opera composer

PENDERECKI, Krzysztof
(ponder•**ets**•key, **cushish**•toff)

b. 1933
Polish composer

PETIPA, Marius
(petty•**paw**)

1819–1910   French dancer, ballet master, creator
of ballets and dominant force in Russian ballet

PETIT, Roland
(puh•**tee**)

b. 1924
French dancer and choreographer

POULENC, Francis
(poo•**lank**)

1899–1963
French composer and pianist

PREY, Herman
(pry)

> *b. 1929*
> *German baritone*

SAINT-SAËNS, Camille
(san•**sawn**, ka•**me**)

> *1835–1921*
> *French composer*

SATIE, Erik
(saw•**tee**)

> *1866–1925*
> *French composer*

SCARLATTI, Domenico
(skar•**lat**•ee)

> *1685–1757*
> *Italian composer and harpsichordist*

SCHOENBERG, Arnold
(**shurn** [preferably with a silent r] burg)

> *1874–1951*
> *Austrian-American composer*

SOLTI, Sir Georg
(**shoal**•tee, george)

> *b. 1912*
> *Hungarian-born orchestra conductor*

SPESSIVTSEVA, Olga
(spes•**eeft**•suh•vah)

> *b. 1895*
> *Russian ballerina*

SZELL, Georg
(sell, George)

> *1897–1970*
> *Hungarian-born conductor*

SZERYNG, Henryk
(**share**•ink)

> *1918–1988*
> *Polish violinist*

SZIGETI, Joseph
(**sig**•etty)

1892–1973
Hungarian-born American violinist

SZYMANOWSKY, Korol
(shim•on•**off**•ski)

1882–1937
Polish composer

VARÈSE, Edgar
(vah•**rez**)

1883–1965
French composer

VIEUXTEMPS, Henri
(view•**tom**)

1820–1881
Belgian composer and violinist

VILLA-LOBOS, Heitor
(vee•lah•**loh**•bohsh, **ay**•tore)

1887–1959
Brazilian composer

VOLLENWEIDER, Andreas
(**foal**•en•vider)

b. 1953
Swiss harpist

WALDTEUFEL, Charles Emile
(**vald**•toy•full)

1837–1915
French composer and pianist

WEBER, Carl Maria von
(**vay**•bur)

1786–1826
German composer

WEBERN, Anton von
(**vay**•burn)

1883–1945
Austrian composer

WEILL, Kurt
(wile)

1900–1950
German-American composer

WEINBERGER, Jaromír
(wine•bare•gur)

1896–1967
Czech composer

WEINGARTNER, Felix
(vine•gartner)

1863–1942
Austrian conductor

WIENIAWSKI, Henri
(veen•yohf•ski)

1835–1880
Polish violinist and composer

WOLF-FERRARI, Ermanno
(volf•fay•rah•ree)

1876–1948
Italian opera composer

YSÄYE, Eugene
(ee•za•ee)

1858–1931
Belgian composer, violinist, conductor

Painting

BAROCCI, Federico
(bah•**rot**•chee)

1535–1612
Italian painter

BAZILLE, Frederic
(bah•**zee**)

1841–1870
French painter

BENOIS, Aleksandr Nikolayevich
(ben•**wah**)

1870–1950   Russian painter best known as a
costume and set designer for the Ballets Russes

BÖCKLIN, Arnold
(**burk**•lin)

1827–1901
Swiss artist

BRAQUE, Georges
(brock, zhorzh)

1882–1963
French painter

BRUEGEL, Peter the Elder
(**broy**•gull)

1525–1569
Flemish painter

CAILLEBOTTE, Gustave
(caw•yuh•**but**)

1848–1894
French painter and art patron

CARAVAGGIO, Michelangelo Merisi da
(cara•**vah**•joe)

1573–1610
Italian painter

CASSATT, Mary
(kuh•**sat**)

1847–1926
American painter

CÉZANNE, Paul
(say•**zahn**)

1839–1906
French painter

CHAGALL, Marc
(shaw•**gall**)

1889–1985
Russian-born painter and designer

CHIRICO, Georgio
(**key**•ree•co, jorjoe)

1888–1978
Italian painter

CIMA da Conegliano
(**chee**•ma)

1459–1517
Italian painter

CIMABUE
(chee•ma•**boo**•ay)

1240–1302
Italian painter. Real name: Cenni de Pepi

CLAESZ, Pieter
(claws)

1597–1661
Dutch painter

COCTEAU, Jean
(cock•**toe**)

1889–1963   French novelist, playwright, poet,
painter, designer and film maker

COROT, Jean Batiste Camille
(co•**roe**)

1796–1875
French painter

CORREGGIO
(co•**red**•joe)

1489–1534
Italian painter. Real name: Antonio Allegri

COURBET, Gustave
(coor•**bay**)

1819–1877
French painter

COUTURE, Thomas
(coo•**tour**)

1815–1879
French painter

COZENS, Alexander
(cousins)

1717–1786
English landscape painter

CRANACH, Lucas the Elder
(**craw**•knock)

1472–1553
German painter

CUYP, Aelbert
(coyp, **al**•bairt)

1620–1691
Dutch painter

DAUBIGNY, Charles Francois
(doe•been•**yee**)

1817–1878
French painter

DAUMIER, Honoré
(dome•ee•**ay**)

1808–1879
French painter and sculptor

DAVID, Jacques Louis
(daw•**veed**)

1748–1825
French painter

DEGAS, Edgar
(duh•**gah**)

1834–1917
French painter

DELACROIX, Eugéne
(de•law•**craw**)

1798–1863
French painter

DELAUNAY, Robert
(duh•low•**nay**, **row**•bare)

1885–1941
French painter

DELVAUX, Paul
(dell•vo)

b. 1897
Belgian painter

DEMUTH, Charles
(**day**•mooth)

1883–1935
American artist

DENIS, Maurice
(duh•**knee**)

1870–1943
French painter

DERAIN, André
(duh•**ran**)

1880–1954
French painter

DIEBENKORN, Richard
(**dee**•ben•corn)

b. 1922
American painter

DORÉ, Gustave
(door•**ay**, goose•tahv)

*1832–1883   French artist famous for wood-
engraved illustrations*

DUBUFFET, Jean
(do•boo•**fay**)

1901–1985
French painter

DUCHAMP, Marcel
(do•**shom**)

1887–1968
French painter

DUFY, Raoul
(do•**fee**, rah•ool)

1887–1953
French painter

DÜRER, Albrecht
(**dyur**•ur, all•brekt)

1471–1528   German artist famous for his
woodcuts and engravings

ERTÉ
(air•**tay**)

1892–1990   Romain de Tirtoff
Russian-born French artist

FANTIN-LATOUR, Henri
(fawn•**tan** law•**tour**)

1836–1904
French painter

FEININGER, Lyonel
(fie•ning•ur)

1871–1956
American artist

FRAGONARD, Jean Honoré
(fraw•go•**nar**)

1732–1806
French painter

FREILICHER, Jane
(**frile**•icker)

b. 1924
American artist

GAUGIN, Paul
(go•**gan**)

1848–1903
French painter

GAULLI, Giovonni Battista
(gah•**ool**•lee)

1639–1709
Italian painter

GÉRICAULT, Théodore
(zhay•re•**co**, tay•o•**door**)

1791–1824
French painter

GÉRÔME, Jean Léon
(zhay•**roam**, zhon **lay**•on)

1824–1904
French painter and sculptor

GIORGIONE
(johr•**joan**•ay)

1477–1510
Italian painter

GIOTTO di Bondone
(**joht**•toe, dee bon•**doe**•nay)

1267–1337
Italian painter

GIOVANNI di Paolo
(joe•**vah**•knee dee **pow**•low)

1403–1482
Sienese painter

GLEIZES, Albert
(glez)

1881–1953
French designer and painter

GOGH, Vincent van
(van•go)

1853–1890
Dutch painter

GRIS, Juan
(grees, whon)

1887–1927
Spanish painter

GROS, Antoine Jean, Baron
(grow)

1771–1835
French painter

GROSZ, George
(gross)

1893–1959
German-American painter

GUÉRIN, Pierre Narcisse, Baron
(gay•ran)

1774–1833
French painter

GUYS, Constantin
(goys)

1805–1892
French painter

HABERLE, John
(haberly)

1856–1933
American painter

HALS, Frans
(halls, frons)

1580–1666
Dutch painter

HECKEL, Erich
(heckle, ay•rick)

1883–1970
German painter

HÉLION, Jean
(ale•yon)

1904–1987
French painter

HEYDEN, Jan Van der
(high•din)

1637–1712
Dutch painter

HOLBEIN, Hans, the Elder
(hole•bine)

1465–1524
German painter

HOOCH, Pieter de
(hock)

1629–1684
Dutch painter

INGRES, Jean Auguste Dominique
(ang•gruh)

1780–1867
French painter

JAWLENSKY, Alexey von
(yow•len•ski)

1864–1941
German expressionist painter

KANDINSKY, Wassily
(kun•dean•ski, vah•see•lee)

1866–1944
Russian-born painter

KIENHOLZ, Edward
(keen•holtz)

b. 1927
American artist

KLEE, Paul
(clay)

1879–1940
Swiss-born painter

KLIMT, Gustav
(kleemt)

1862–1918
Austrian painter

KOKOSCHKA, Oskar
(co•**cosh**•kuh, **ohs**•kur)

1896–1980
Austrian-born painter, poet and playwright

KOLLWITZ, Käthe
(**cawl**•vits, **kay**•tuh)

1867–1945
German graphic artist

LANDSEER, Sir Edwin
(**lan**•seer)

1802–1873
English painter

LÉGER, Fernand
(lay•**zhay**, fair•**non**)

1881–1955
French painter

LICHTENSTEIN, Roy
(**lick**•ten•steen)

b. 1923
American artist

LURCAT, Jean
(lure•**sah**, zhawn)

1892–1966
French painter and designer

MAGRITTE, René
(muh•**greet**)

1898–1967
Belgian painter

MANET, Édouard
(maw•**nay**, ay•**dwahr**)

1832–1883
French painter

MARISOL
(**mare**•eye•sull)

b. 1930   American pop artist of Venezuelan
ancestry. Full name: Marisol Escobar

MICHELANGELO
(mickle•**an**•jullo)

*1475–1564   Italian sculptor and painter. Last
name: Buonarotti*

MILLAIS, Sir John Everett
(mill•ay)

*1829–1896
British painter*

MILLET, Jean Francois
(me•**lay**)

*1814–1875
French painter*

MINNE, George
(min, zhorzh)

*1866–1941
Belgian painter and sculptor*

MIRÓ, Joan
(me•**roe**, hoe•**on**)

*1893–1983
Spanish painter*

MODIGLIANI, Amadeo
(mo•deal•ee•**ah**•knee)

*1884–1920
Italian painter and sculptor*

MOHOLY-NAGY, Lázló
(**mo**•holy•**nod**•yuh, laws•low)

*1895–1946   Hungarian-born painter, sculptor,
stage designer, photographer and film maker*

MONDRIAN, Piet
(**moan**•dree•on, peet)

*1872–1944
Dutch painter*

MONET, Claude
(mow•**nay**, cload)

*1890–1926
French painter*

MORISOT, Berthe
(more•ee•zoh, bairt)

> *1841–1895   French painter, the first woman associated with Impressionism*

MUNCH, Edvard
(moonk, **ed**•vart)

> *1863–1944*
> *Norwegian painter*

PAOLOZZI, Eduardo
(pow•**lot**•see)

> *b. 1924*
> *Scottish artist*

PECHSTEIN, Max
(**peck**•shtine)

> *1881–1955*
> *German painter and print maker*

RAPHAEL
(rah•fah•**el**)

> *1483–1520*
> *Italian painter*

RAUSCHENBERG, Robert
(**row** [as in brow]•shan•burg)

> *b. 1925*
> *American artist*

ROUAULT, George
(roo•**oh**)

> *1871–1958*
> *French painter*

RUSCHA, Edward
(roo•**shay**)

> *b. 1937*
> *American artist*

SCHIELE, Egon
(**she**•luh)

> *1890–1918*
> *Austrian painter*

SCHWITTERS, Kurt
(**shvit**•urs)

1887–1948
German artist

SEURAT, Georges
(sir•**ah**)

1859–1891
French painter

SIGNAC, Paul
(seen•**yawk**)

1863–1935
French painter

SISLEY, Alfred
(sees•**lay**)

1839–1899
French painter

SOULAGES, Pierre
(sue•**lawzh**)

b. 1919
French painter

SOUTINE, Chaim
(sue•**teen**, kye•im)

1893–1943
Russian-born painter

TANGUY, Yves
(tawn•**gee** [as in geek], eve)

1910–1955
French painter

TOULOUSE-LAUTREC, Henri de
(too•**looz**, low•**trek**)

1864–1901
French artist

UTRILLO, Maurice
(oo•**tree**•oh)

1883–1955
French painter

VAN GOGH, Vincent
(van go)

1853–1890
Dutch painter

VASARELY, Victor
(vah•zah•ray•**lee**)

b. 1908
Hungarian artist

VELÁZQUEZ, Diego
(veh•**lass**•kez)

1599–1660
*Spanish painter (Spanish: vay•**lawth**•kayth)*

VERMEER, Jan
(ver•**mayr**)

1632–1675
Dutch painter

VERONESE, Paolo
(vay•roh•**nay**•zay)

1528–1588
Italian painter

VUILLARD, Édouard
(vwee•**yar**)

1868–1940
French artist

Sculpture

BARLACH, Ernst
(**bar**•lock)

1870–1939
German sculptor, artist and dramatist

BARTHOLDI, Frédéric Auguste
(bar•toll•**dee**)

1834–1904
French sculptor

BARYE, Antoine Louis
(bar•**ree**)

1796–1875
French sculptor

BERTOIA, Harry
(bare•**toy**•uh)

1915–1978
Italian-born American sculptor

BRANCUSI, Constantin
(brong•**coo**•zee)

1876–1957
Rumanian-born sculptor

CARO, Anthony
(**car**•o)

b. 1924
English sculptor

CELLINI, Benvenuto
(chell•**lee**•knee)

1500–1571
Italian sculptor, goldsmith, architect and writer

CÉSAR
(say•**zar**)

b. 1924
French sculptor. Christened César Baldaccini

COYSEVOX, Antoine
(quaz•**vo**)

1640–1720
French sculptor

DAUMIER, Honoré
(dome•ee•**ay**)

1808–1879
French painter and sculptor

FALCONET, Étienne Maurice
(fall•co•**nay**)

1716–1791
French sculptor

FLAVIN, Dan
(**flay**•vin)

b. 1933   American artist famous for abstract
neon sculptures

GABO, Naum
(**gah**•bo, nowm)

1890–1977
Russian-American sculptor, painter and architect

GARGALLO, Pablo
(gar•**gall**•yo)

1881–1934
Spanish sculptor

GAUDIER-BRZESKA, Henri
(go•dee•**ay**, bur•zes•**ka**)

1891–1915
French sculptor

GÉRÔME, Jean Léon
(zhay•**roam**, zhon **lay**•on)

1824–1904
French painter and sculptor

GHIBERTI, Lorenzo
(gee [as in geek]•**bare**•tee)

1381–1455
Italian sculptor

GIACOMETTI, Alberto
(jacko•**met**•tee)

1901–1966
Swiss sculptor

GOERITZ, Mathias
(**gur**•its)

b. 1951
German sculptor and architect living in Mexico

GROSS, Chaim
(kime)

b. 1904
Czech-born American sculptor

HAAKE, Hans
(**haw**•kuh)

b. 1936
German-born U.S. sculptor/artist

KOLBE, Georg
(**coal**•buh, gay•**ork**)

1877–1947
German sculptor

LIPCHITZ, Jacques
(leep•**sheets**, zhock)

1891–1973
Lithuanian-born French sculptor

MAILLOL, Aristide
(my•**ohl**, ar•ees•**teed**)

1861–1944
French sculptor and graphic artist

MICHELANGELO
(mickle•**an**•jullo)

*1475–1564   Italian sculptor and painter. Last
name: Buonarotti*

MILLES, Carl
(**mill**•iss)

1875–1955
Swedish-American sculptor

MINNE, George
(min, zhorzh)

1866–1941
Belgian painter and sculptor

MODIGLIANI, Amadeo
(mo•deal•ee•ah•knee)

1884–1920
Italian painter and sculptor

MOHOLY-NAGY, Lázló
(**mo**•holy•**nod**•yuh, laws•low)

1895–1946   Hungarian-born painter, sculptor,
stage designer, photographer and film maker

ROSZAK, Theodore
(**raw**•shock)

b. 1907
American sculptor and painter

STANKIEWICZ, Richard
(**stang**•key•e•vich)

b. 1922
American sculptor

TINGUELY, Jean
(tan•**glee**)

1925–1991
Swiss sculptor

Index

By alphabetical order

Graphic Design by:
Herman Design Group, Inc.

Typeset by:
Coghill Composition Company,
Richmond, Virginia
in Garamond Bold Condensed
and Garamond Book Cond. Italic
Litho in U.S.A.